HEN PARTY

planning

GUIDE L

Verity Davidson

summersdale

C000164426

HEN PARTY PLANNING GUIDE

Copyright © Summersdale Publishers Ltd, 2016

Research by Emily Kearns

All rights reserved.

No part of this book may be reproduced by any means, nor transmitted, nor translated into a machine language, without the written permission of the publishers.

Condition of Sale
This book is sold subject to the condition that it shall not, by way of trade or otherwise, be lent, resold, hired out or otherwise circulated in any form of binding or cover other than that in which it is published and without a similar condition including this condition being imposed on the subsequent purchaser.

Summersdale Publishers Ltd
46 West Street
Chichester
West Sussex
PO19 1RP
UK

www.summersdale.com

Printed and bound in Malta

ISBN: 978-1-84953-892-3

Substantial discounts on bulk quantities of Summersdale books are available to corporations, professional associations and other organisations. For details contact Nicky Douglas by telephone: +44 (0) 1243 756902, fax: +44 (0) 1243 786300 or email: nicky@summersdale.com.

CONTENTS

INTRODUCTION

So you've been tasked with organising a hen party. Are you the sole organiser? Do you have helpers? Are you in charge of five or 35 hens? Does the bride-to-be want to go abroad, for a week? A weekend? Does she want to keep it local and just go to a nearby pub and for a bite to eat at a restaurant a stone's throw from where she lives? Or maybe she wants to head to a cottage in the country for a weekend of games and to immerse herself in nature? Perhaps you are the bride and you'd rather organise things yourself. There are many decisions to be made!

The number of guests and desired activities will greatly affect the amount of work required of you, the organiser. Organising a hen party might look like hard work, but it should ultimately be enjoyable – if you start to feel stressed you may find you need an extra pair of hands to help out. Don't be afraid to ask the bride-to-be to designate another helper if you're feeling overwhelmed.

The information and advice in the following pages will help you to make these decisions, and suggest various themes and activities for different personality types, not to mention a host of games and cocktail recipes that could help to shape your weekend.

Without further ado, it's time to get planning!

MAKING A PLAN

'FAIL TO PLAN,
PLAN TO FAIL.'
★ *Hillary Clinton* ★

Is your bride-to-be likely to turn her nose up at the stereotypical hen party L-plates and inflatable penises? Or does she enjoy that sort of silliness, even if only ironically? The chances are you know well enough whether she would prefer an evening of crafting and sipping cocktails out of teacups over strutting her stuff in a banging nightclub while sporting a veil adorned with condom packets and a brightly coloured sash announcing her impending marital status.

We all like to party in different ways and find comfort in varying activities and attires – stick with what you know and what you know she would want. Whether that's a cheese and wine tasting followed by a scavenger hunt, or pole-dancing lessons followed by a yard of shots, there's something here for every scenario. Put her first, but don't forget about the other guests. If half of them suffer from vertigo, for example, don't arrange a weekend of high-wire-type activities that would see much of the two days spent at great height.

Take one step at a time and it'll all come together.

SIT DOWN WITH THE BRIDE-TO-BE

Before you do anything else, sit down with the bride-to-be and come up with a few potential dates for the hen party. Do this as far in advance as possible – the more notice you give the guests, the more likely most of them will be able to make it. And when it comes to booking accommodation, activities and travel, you want to get in there before everything is booked up.

Ask the bride-to-be for a rough idea of what she'd like to do – does she want to go abroad or stay closer to home? What sort of weekend does she have in mind? Classy and potentially a little pricey, or cheap and cheerful and to a strict budget?

HOW TO SORT THE GUEST LIST

Talk to the bride-to-be about who she would like to share her hen party with. Does she want mothers in attendance, for example? This might affect the, ahem, surprises you 'inflict' on her over the course of the hen party. Or then again, it might not. Are there any guests who don't get along with each other? How to best handle this should be discussed with the bride-to-be. The number of guests will also affect the activities you can plan for the group, so it's good to get this all sorted as far in advance as possible.

Once you've got a clear idea of what kind of event it's going to be, gather the contact details of all those invited (the bride-to-be should be able to supply you with these) and send out a 'save the date' invitation. Introduce yourself, let them know they have been invited to a hen party and add a sentence or two about what that might entail. Ask them to RSVP by a certain date – a week or two in the future should give them enough time – and chase them if they haven't replied by this date.

HOW TO CONTACT GUESTS

★ Email

★ Letter with perforated RSVP

★ Postcard with picture of the bride-to-be

★ Social media group

★ WhatsApp group

★ Group text message

★ Cookie/marshmallow with date iced/printed on it

★ Pop-up card themed to bride-to-be

★ Balloon with date printed on it

Rather than finding your inbox flooded with RSVPs from hens, ask them to fill in a quick and simple online poll to determine who is available and when. Doodle.com is a good tool for this: simply follow the instructions, add the potential

party dates and email the link to the hens. Once everyone has filled it in, you'll be able to see which dates are the most popular and when would be best to hold the party.

SAMPLE EMAIL TO HENS

Dear Hens,

Some of you know me, but for those who don't – Hi! I'm [insert bride-to-be's name here]'s best friend/sister/bridesmaid and have been asked to sort out her hen party, to which you have been invited.

We're looking at a few dates in [insert month(s) here] and it would be great if you could follow this link and let me know your availability [insert Doodle poll link here].

[Insert bride-to-be's name here] is keen to spend a weekend in [a cottage/European destination]/[holiday resort – delete/add as applicable] and would love for you to join in on the fun ahead of her big day.

I hope you can make it and look forward to hearing from you.

[insert your name here]

BUDGET

Decide on a budget with the bride-to-be – be sensible – if the hens earn wildly varying amounts, be sympathetic to that and keep it cheap. The ones who earn loads can buy in the bubbly if they want to make an extra contribution.

MAKE RULES AND STICK TO THEM

★ Decide whether or not a ban should be placed on uploading photos ('risky' or not) to the internet.

★ Perhaps the hens should 'buddy up' to stop each other from drunk-dialling or uploading aforementioned banned photos to the internet.

★ In the unlikely event that anyone falls out with the bride-to-be or you notice tension building – for example a disgruntled wannabe bridesmaid who's had one cocktail too many – be ready to defuse the situation. This is the bride-to-be's special weekend and a hen party ruckus will never be forgotten.

HOW MUCH TO TELL THE BRIDE-TO-BE

Make sure you are clear on how much the bride-to-be wants to know about the weekend and what she would prefer to be kept as a surprise. She may want to be involved every step of the way, in which case you might want to organise some smaller surprises – maybe a special outfit for her to wear or a gift from all her hens. Above all, make sure any surprises will go down well – that may mean sounding out any ideas with her sister, mother or the other hens just to make sure.

CHECKLIST

Before you do anything else, make a list of what needs to be done and in what order. Your list should look something like this:

- ☐ Decide possible dates with bride-to-be

- ☐ Gather list of hens' contact details from bride-to-be

- ☐ Send out an email to hens to check they are available

- ☐ Sit down with the bride-to-be to discuss particulars

- ☐ Do your research

- ☐ Communicate with the guests about budget/loose plans so far

- ☐ Do some more research with the above in mind

- [ ] Set a detailed budget
- [ ] Book accommodation and gather funds from hens
- [ ] Book activities and gather funds from hens
- [ ] Assign jobs to other hens, if needs be
- [ ] Send out an itinerary and accommodation details, including requests for any props, etc. the hens need to bring with them
- [ ] Send an email to all the hens the week before the event, just to check everyone is prepared and has all the information they need.

THEMES

THEME: SOPHISTICATED

'SIMPLICITY IS THE ULTIMATE SOPHISTICATION.'

★ *Leonardo da Vinci* ★

For the more sophisticated bride-to-be and her entourage, how about a weekend at a spa hotel or a luxury cottage? A decadent weekend escape and a focus on relaxation isn't a bad shout when back at home she will no doubt be up to her eyeballs in table plans and bouquet brochures. There's still room for fun, however – pair the relaxation with some of the below activities.

DAYTIME ACTIVITIES

Hire a beautician/masseuse – If you choose the luxury cottage option, bring the pampering with you and lay on facials, massages, manicures and pedicures mere steps away from where you had breakfast. Get the hens to sign up and pay for specific treatments beforehand so you can book the required number of miracle workers to perform your treatments.

Sushi-making workshop – Not only a fun activity, but a valuable insight into how to correctly prepare the popular Japanese cuisine. You'll learn how to cook sushi rice, what types of fish to use, a teacher will provide all the kit and you'll get to taste your creations once you've finished. If you want to take it one step further, why not ask your teacher to recommend a few different sakes for you to taste as you go or to pair with the sushi. (Remember: Check if any of the hens are vegetarian, pregnant or harbour a hatred of raw fish before booking this activity!)

Afternoon tea – Many hotels and restaurants offer various afternoon tea packages – from the simple tea and cake, to gallons of tea, mountains of cake and sandwiches, and champagne cocktails to boot. A pleasant and decadent way to spend an afternoon, relaxing and gorging, and catching up with/getting to know the other hens. For something a bit different, opt for a themed Mad Hatter's Tea Party-style affair.

Perfume-making experience – This activity will see all the hens have something special to take home with them. Sessions for hen party groups will involve being guided by experts 'on a sensory journey' to create your own unique blend. Help the bride-to-be create a scent that she can wear on her wedding day and remember the process for years to come.

Learn the Charleston – If your hens are up for learning something new and strutting their stuff to some vintage tunes, then learning the Charleston might be a good idea. An organised dance class will teach hens some classic moves, and most will provide props such as beads and feathers.

HEN HACK

For a **pampering party** on a budget, bring all the kit with you. Ask each hen for a small contribution and load up on face masks, manicure and pedicure sets, different-coloured nail polish and even disposable spa slippers. Ask each hen to bring their own dressing gown, pour everyone a glass of bubbly while they pamper themselves and take it in turns to do each other's nails.

EVENING ACTIVITIES

Wine-tasting experience – You'll find yourself spoilt for choice when searching for wine tasting experiences and packages. Head out to a bar or wine tasting centre or bring an expert in house if you've hired a cottage. They'll teach you how to taste and appreciate a few different wines, and you could even ask them to pair the different wines with various nibbles or cheeses, for example, to keep all hens' stomachs sufficiently lined!

Gin-tasting experience – The current gin renaissance means there are a lot of gin tasting activities to choose from, too. Is your bride-to-be partial to the odd G&T? Arrange a gin tasting for your hens and learn about the various botanicals that create the flavours in the different examples, and the garnishes that complement them.

Themed cocktail party – A cocktail party themed around, say, *The Great Gatsby* could be just what the sophisticated bride-to-be ordered. Perhaps you've kept this a surprise from her, or perhaps you haven't, but arrange for the other hens to bring 1920s fancy dress and props, feathers, beads and sparkly attire, and something for the bride-to-be to wear, and serve bubbly in 1920s coupe champagne glasses. And you can all crack out those Charleston moves you have been honing.

HEN HACK

Afternoon tea is another classic hen party activity that can be made much cheaper if you need to keep costs down. If you're staying in a cottage, or if there is no accommodation involved and hens are meeting at the bride-to-be's or one of the bridesmaids' homes, host your own version of afternoon tea. Grab a cake stand or two from a charity shop and load them up with crust-less sandwiches, cakes and scones (provide clotted cream and jam for a decadent cream tea). Borrow a teapot and teacups if you don't already have them and ask around the hens for the right number of champagne flutes so no one goes empty handed. Garnish each glass of bubbly with a fresh strawberry and you'll wonder why anyone bothers shelling out for afternoon tea when you can do it this well at home!

ESSENTIAL KIT

★ Pampering essentials
★ Cocktail glasses

FANCY DRESS IDEAS

★ 1920s flapper
★ A day at the races
★ Hollywood glamour

THEME: OUTDOORS

'SUNSHINE IS DELICIOUS, RAIN IS REFRESHING, WIND BRACES US UP, SNOW IS EXHILARATING; THERE IS REALLY NO SUCH THING AS BAD WEATHER, ONLY DIFFERENT KINDS OF GOOD WEATHER.'

★ *John Ruskin* ★

If your bride-to-be loves nature and the outdoors, then a weekend of glamping or relaxing in a forest cabin could be just the thing. Surrounded by lush countryside, with a plethora of walking trails, scenery and outdoor pursuits, there will be plenty to occupy all the hens in the daytime, and at the end of it they'll be able to sit around a big campfire to play games. And if the budget allows, opt for a forest cabin with a hot tub so your hens can soak under the stars with a glass in hand – the ultimate luxury. String up bunting and battery-operated fairy lights around the tents or cabins to create a magical feel.

DAYTIME ACTIVITIES

Bird-handling experience – There are birds of prey centres all over the country where you can spend an afternoon with an expert and meet, hold and feed the birds. From falcons to eagles and all sorts of owls, if the bride-to-be is an animal lover then this will go down a treat. Check that none of your hens have a bird phobia before booking this activity!

Hiking – When in beautiful lush green scenery, and with good weather, outdoor types will be happy to pull on their hiking boots and head out into the fresh air. Opt for a walk with interesting features, which is suitable for all, isn't 12 miles long and has a pub at the end of it – that will keep everyone happy. You can make things more exciting by introducing a treasure hunt element to the hike. Don't forget you'll have to organise this in advance, however. Head online to find information on footpaths and trails, and don't forget to take your mobiles and an old-school paper map to make sure everyone gets back safely.

Horse-riding – If you happen to have a particularly horse-mad group of hens, then a hack through the countryside might be worth considering. Make sure the accommodation you choose has plenty of bridleways nearby and a riding centre that will be able to provide horses that are suitable for all the hens, taking into account their levels of experience.

HEN HACK

Organise a **scavenger hunt** or treasure hunt, or send the hens geocaching (www.geocaching.com) for money-saving fun. Hen parties don't have to be expensive and, as long as it isn't pouring with rain or snowing, there is plenty of free fun to be had outdoors. If you want to arrange a scavenger hunt, you'll have to visit the area ahead of the weekend itself (or at least be familiar with it) in order to tailor the hunt to the location. Grab a bottle of cheap bubbly to offer as a first prize.

EVENING ACTIVITIES

Night hike – A night hike can be fun and a bit spooky, especially if it involves tramping through woods. Make sure you do a bit of research first to ensure it's safe to do this – paths are wide and there are no sheer drops, etc. Also make sure all hens are well equipped with wellies and torches. Depending on your group's scaredy-cat threshold, tell ghost stories while you're hiking in the dark.

Games – If you're staying under canvas, you might find the best use of your evening involves a whole lot of game playing around a campfire. A good campfire game is Fantasy Music Festival. Take it in turns to go around the circle, each saying 'I'm going to a music festival, let me tell you who's going to be there…' The first person should say an artist/band beginning with A, for example Abba, the second person should then say 'I'm going to a music festival, let me tell you who's going to be there… Abba, Blur…' and so on until the end of the alphabet. If anyone forgets a band/artist give them a forfeit.

Eat s'mores – Channel your inner American camper and take campfire marshmallows to the next level with traditional s'mores. You will need: marshmallows, a large bar of milk chocolate, sweet biscuits (plain digestives or rich tea will do) and some long wooden skewers. Grab a plate and two biscuits, add a square of chocolate to one of the biscuits and toast one or two marshmallows over the flames. Once suitably bubbling (but not black!), transfer the mallow goo to one of your biscuits and place the other on top – now enjoy the true camper's night-time sandwich.

HEN HACK

Some people loathe camping, but no one can deny that luxury camping, or glamping, is a comfortable and affordable way to pass a fun weekend. If your hens are on a budget or you're trying to keep costs down, opt for a weekend under luxury canvas and **create your own festival** vibe with a playlist of the bride-to-be's favourite songs, beer or wine in plastic cups (BYO is a huge money saver), a big campfire or fire pit and you could even send invitations that look like tickets and name the 'event' after the bride-to-be. If your budget doesn't stretch to glamping, perhaps you could arrange to go to a normal campsite but bring along the luxuries you might not usually enjoy – such as airbeds and duvets – as well as your sleeping bag. A small contribution from each of the hens would see you able to afford a large tent that could act as a lounging area, in which you could all hang out and play games, should you desire. Pitch this next to your sleeping tents and there'll always be somewhere to socialise, come rain or shine.

ESSENTIAL KIT

★ S'mores ingredients

★ Bunting and battery-operated fairy lights

★ Sensible clothes and shoes

FANCY DRESS IDEAS

★ Musical legends

★ Forest creatures

★ *A Midsummer Night's Dream*

★ The *Lord of the Rings*

THEME: ACTIVE

**'ADVENTURE IS
WORTHWHILE IN ITSELF.'**

★ *Amelia Earhart* ★

If your band of hens are sporty types, fans of the outdoors and like to be active whenever possible, why not try a weekend on a canal boat for something a bit different, or a holiday village or adventure park? Depending on the budget and time of year, if the bride-to-be is a keen winter sports enthusiast, you might want to think about surprising her with a weekend in the snow – either real or artificial.

DAYTIME ACTIVITIES

Water sports – If you're near the coast, there are plenty of options from surfing lessons to kayaking, coasteering, kitesurfing or paddleboarding, and there's always bodyboarding or swimming/paddling for the less confident or novice hens. Depending on location, you might find the thrill of white-water rafting is just the thing for your hens. Even if you're miles from any significant body of water, there is likely to be a water sports centre in the vicinity that will offer water skiing or sailing.

Tank driving – Always wanted to drive a tank? Well now is your chance. Various companies offer this as an experience, where hens can drive tanks around a purpose-built circuit. Some of these tanks are mini one-person versions, while others will fit several of your hens in for a rough and muddy ride.

Aerial acrobatics – If your hens have a head for heights, why not have a go at an aerial acrobatics class complete with aerial hoops, silks, slings and trapezes. Not only is this great for strengthening one's muscles, but it's something a bit different and fun that active hens will enjoy.

Hula-hooping – For the energetic hens, why not have a go at a hula-hooping class, where you can not only learn the art of hula-hooping, including several different moves, but also strengthen your core and have fun at the same time. Companies offer various themes, including Hawaiian.

Snowboarding/skiing – If your bride-to-be has a penchant for snow sports, this could be a great idea. If your budget can stretch that far and the ski season is in full swing, you could look into heading to the mountains for a (long) weekend. For a more affordable option, which can be just as fun, head to an artificial snow dome and spend a day racing down the artificial slopes.

Paintballing – For the brave and competitive hens who enjoy a good old run around, a game of paintballing could be just the ticket. Make sure you have the right number of hens for an activity like this, otherwise you may end up being shot at by strangers – which might seem a bit more menacing and take the fun out of it all somewhat!

HEN HACK

If you're looking for budget options, do you have a friend or fellow hen who might be able or willing to lead a **dance class** for you for a lesser fee? Perhaps you know someone who is a personal trainer or is an experienced hula hooper, or even simply a good dancer and is happy to teach everyone a routine to perform at the wedding.

EVENING ACTIVITIES

Dancing – If your hens aren't absolutely burnt-out from all the activities of the day, then now could be the time to put those skills learnt earlier to the test and head out dancing. Depending on your location – a cottage or log cabin in the depths of the countryside might not provide an ideal spot close to some banging nightlife – either head into town for a night on the tiles (phone ahead to check they accept large groups) or make the party happen where you are. Close all the curtains, dim the lights and encourage your hens to challenge each other to a dance-off.

Beer pong – Combining beer and ball sports – what could go wrong? This American college drinking game is a game of skill and perfect for this sort of hen party. If no one likes beer just use fruity cider or alcopops instead. You'll need a long table, 20 large plastic cups (if you want to be authentic, go for the red ones), several ping-pong balls and plenty of beer (or your drink of choice). Arrange ten cups in a triangle at the end of each table, as you would arrange the balls at the start of a game of pool. Fill each cup half-full with beer – or a quarter-full, if you want to pace yourselves a bit (advisable if not playing in teams!). Fill a bucket with clean water and set to one side – this is for cleaning the ping-pong balls when they bounce and roll under sofas. The aim of the game is to throw a ping-pong ball into your opponent's cup – if you're successful, they will have to drink its contents. Continue like this until one side has no cups left – whoever drinks all their beer first loses.

HEN HACK

Instead of getting an expert in to teach you how to **make cocktails**, save some pennies by making the cocktails yourselves, teaching the other hens as you go. With a little easy research and a few bits of kit, you can add theatre and flair to the simplest of creations. Take a look at the Cocktail Recipes chapter for some inspiration. You can have fun coming up with silly names for them – double entendres are entirely optional, of course.

ESSENTIAL KIT

★ Muscle soak bubble bath/Deep Heat

★ Outdoor clothes

★ Sensible shoes

★ Beer pong ingredients

★ Dancing shoes

FANCY DRESS IDEAS

★ Famous sportspeople

★ Outfits inspired by bride-to-be's initials

★ Cocktail names

★ Circus performers

THEME: CREATIVE

'IT IS A CURIOUS THOUGHT,
BUT IT IS ONLY WHEN
YOU SEE PEOPLE LOOKING
RIDICULOUS THAT YOU
REALISE JUST HOW MUCH
YOU LOVE THEM.'

★ *Agatha Christie* ★

Creative hens might like the idea of a weekend away somewhere with some character. Why not look to stay in a treehouse or some vintage gypsy caravans at a campsite? You could also look at bell tents, luxury yurts and themed cottages or B&Bs. The creative hen will be open to learning a new skill, perhaps crafting her way through the weekend. Be aware of everyone's skills and choose activities that are easy for the novice to master.

DAYTIME ACTIVITIES

Life drawing – Perfect for arty hens and a good icebreaker for those who don't know the whole group. There are many life-drawing classes specifically tailored to hens for you to choose from and they cater for novices, too. Specialist companies will send a tutor and model (who will remove all of his clothes, yes) to where you're staying and provide you with all the drawing materials and guidance you need, false moustache and beret included. Perhaps double-check that everyone will be comfortable with the amount of bare flesh involved in such a session before booking.

Vintage knicker making – Various crafting companies offer vintage knicker-making classes so each hen leaves with a special memento of the day and the newfound skill to create more pairs should she so desire. Some providers accompany the afternoon of knicker-making fun with a retro-inspired champagne cream tea.

Jewellery making – With some expert guidance your hens could sit down to an afternoon of jewellery making and potentially make something to wear on the big day, while learning a new skill in the process. Lots of experience-led events organisers offer tutored classes and will supply all the sparkly materials required to make items of your choice, from necklaces and earrings, to bracelets and hair slides.

Fascinator making – This is a great idea if the hens are up for creating something they can wear on the big day. Various crafty companies offer fascinator-making workshops and will provide all the materials, and talk you through the various styles and techniques you need to create a unique piece of headwear. Or why not combine an afternoon of fascinator constructing with a tea party on the side?

HEN HACK

If these crafting classes are beyond your budget, you could always look at buying in some **crafting kits** or, if you're feeling brave or creative enough, gather the materials yourself. Many craft retailers offer ready-made crafting party kits for jewellery, fascinator, garter, lantern and bunting making, not to mention knicker customisation, which will make your planning even simpler.

EVENING ACTIVITIES

Vintage dress-up with cocktail party – Add a touch of vintage glamour to your weekend and bring in a vintage make-up and hair specialist to pamper you all and teach you some retro styles. Get yourselves dolled up in vintage gear and hold a cocktail party, serving drinks and canapés, and use vintage teacups or cocktail glasses for maximum effect. Don't forget to take photographs of all the hens in their vintage finery.

Pizza making: Kill two birds with one stone by turning dinner into your evening's entertainment. Buy some pizza bases and an array of toppings and sauces, and spend the night making and enjoying your culinary creations. To spice things up, you could hold a competition for the most inventive pizza, the tastiest flavour combination, or the wackiest design. Alternatively, various pizza establishments may also offer pizza-making experiences, so you can get your hands dirty, but not your kitchen!

Swing dancing – If you've gone for the vintage makeover, it's likely you're up for a spot of swing dancing. Bring in an expert and learn all the moves before going out on the tiles, dressed to impress, to show them off. Check your local listings to find providers of dance classes that will see you working the floor like it's 1929.

HEN HACK

Hold an **upcycling party**. Arrange for the hens to bring along unwanted items of clothing – stuff that was bound for the charity shop bag. For a very small contribution from each hen, make it your job to supply scraps of material and a load of cheap sequins, buttons, threads and glue etc. Organise for one or two hens to bring sewing machines for those who are feeling ambitious. If no one wants to chop up old clothes, buy some very cheap plain items of clothing and decorate them with the aforementioned supplies and fabric pens, etc. The idea is everyone will wear their creations to a party in the evening. Be as creative as possible for optimum effect.

ESSENTIAL KIT

★ Dancing shoes

★ Best singing voice

★ Craft supplies

FANCY DRESS IDEAS

★ Vintage glamour

★ Upcycled chic (or not)

★ Famous artists

★ Subjects of famous paintings/works of art

THEME: CULTURED

'IF YOU OBEY ALL THE RULES, YOU MISS ALL THE FUN.'

★ *Katharine Hepburn* ★

Choose a literary destination for your celebration – somewhere like Bath, Haworth, Stratford-upon-Avon or Whitby in the UK, for example. What is the bride-to-be's favourite book or author? If the author is British, perhaps you can tailor the weekend to this. For example, if she's a huge Brontë fan, you could head to the Haworth in West Yorkshire and spend an afternoon walking the Yorkshire moors, the inspiration for *Wuthering Heights*, as well as exploring the town and stopping at the local pub their brother Branwell used to frequent. Alternatively, Jane Austen fans may enjoy a weekend in Bath, where the author lived for several years, and visit the museum or even the Jane Austen Festival; or there's always Torquay for Agatha Christie fans, Stratford-upon-Avon for followers of Shakespeare or the Lake District for fans of the great poets. And don't forget Whitby, the birthplace of Bram Stoker's *Dracula*, for a weekend with a darker edge. Alternatively, budget permitting, you could head to Paris, Rome, Tallinn, Prague, Seville, Budapest or Barcelona to soak up a weekend of culture and history.

DAYTIME ACTIVITIES

Scavenger hunt – A plethora of companies offer both ready-made and tailor-made scavenger hunts for large groups, relevant to your chosen location. A cheaper alternative is to come up with the hunt yourself, or alternatively write a quiz that relates to the hen weekend destination, which would involve the hens having to explore the town/city to answer all the questions. Throw in a few sets of questions relevant to the bride-to-be and test her guests' knowledge of their friend.

Kimono party – This is your chance to live and learn about Japanese culture and its rituals, while dressed in traditional kimono and *kanzashi* (hair ornaments). All hens will be dressed and styled, each will be given a Japanese name and its meaning, and taught how to write it using calligraphy, as well as learning how to make sushi and how to perform the ancient tea ceremony. Check your local listings for specialist companies offering a kimono experience.

Food festival – With various food and drink festivals taking place throughout the year you'll have no trouble finding something to suit your date and location. What better way to pass an afternoon than wandering around food and drink stalls and sampling the fare on offer. Many food festivals also provide entertainment.

EVENING ACTIVITIES

Flash-fiction writing – Do you have a bunch of budding writers in the group? Or a bride-to-be who is herself something of a scribe or has an interest in it? Do I hear a yes? Send all the hens off to put pen to paper for 30–45 minutes only and come up with a 300–500-word piece of fiction that stars the bride-to-be as a central character. (Perhaps the bride-to-be can write a piece of fiction about her husband-to-be.) When the time is up, all hens should reconvene, pour everyone a drink and take it in turns to read out their creations. The funnier the better! The best thing about this activity is that it is 100 per cent free and can be loads of fun. If you'd rather skip the fiction, opt for a true story involving the writer and the bride-to-be – again, the funnier the better and get everyone to be as descriptive as possible.

Wine/gin tasting – A wine and cheese tasting or a gin tasting with a history lesson thrown in could be just the ticket for cultured hens who aren't mad about throwing luminous-coloured shots down their throats. A quick search online will lead you to a wealth of companies offering various wine tasting event packages where hens have the chance to sample a selection of wines and will be taught how to taste them like a pro. If the bride-to-be is more of a gin drinker, look into a group gin tasting – either in a venue or at your accommodation – led by trained mixologists.

HEN HACK

Create a **pub quiz** with a difference – this one is also a pub crawl but no one knows where to, yet. You might need a bit of help and/or forward planning for this one. Select four or five pubs in the town or city where you are spending your weekend; write general knowledge questions, or ones relevant to the bride-to-be's interests, and ensure the first letter of each answer will spell out the name of the next pub when read down the page. This takes a bit of work – but it's worth it! You'll have to either make sure you're always at the next pub to hand over the next quiz sheet or sweet talk a member of the bar staff into handing it over for you. Make sure you're in the last pub with a bottle of bubbly to award to the team who makes it there first.

ESSENTIAL KIT

★ Quiz hat
★ Guidebook
★ Writing materials

FANCY DRESS IDEAS

★ Famous authors (living or dead)
★ Heroes and villains
★ Song titles
★ Literary characters

THEME: OUTGOING

'THE MODERN HENS' WEEKEND IS A FAIRY TALE EXPERIENCE ALL RIGHT — SCRIPTED BY THE BROTHERS GRIMM.'

★ *Kathy Lette* ★

Perhaps you've opted to rent a house in a city for the weekend or you're staying in a hotel or B & B on the outskirts. Whatever your decision, for this sort of hen party it's likely you'll need to be close to the action. Perhaps your bride-to-be is an avid clubber or a karaoke queen, who likes nothing more than to rent a private karaoke booth with her friends on a Friday night before heading off to paint the town all shades of red. If this is the case, then a quiet country cottage is unlikely to be your best bet. Pick a spot with plenty of nightlife and clubs to suit your bride-to-be's musical tastes, not to mention plenty of options when it comes to daytime activities.

DAYTIME ACTIVITIES

Trip to a theme park – Wherever you choose to go, there is likely to be a theme park nearby to sate the adrenaline-junkie bride-to-be's appetite. Theme parks have plenty to offer adult groups and some even offer onsite accommodation in case one day of being flung about on rollercoasters isn't enough.

Recording studio experience – Is the bride-to-be a born performer? If so, why not investigate hiring a recording studio for a day or afternoon. Not only will she feel like a star for the day, you could also lay down some tracks for her to keep as a memento of the weekend. Better still, get together with the other hens ahead of the weekend and write a song about the bride for you all to perform and record for her on the day. Set the lyrics to a well-known tune and if there are no musical types in the group, get in touch with the studio and ask them to provide a backing track.

Pole dancing – Perhaps your bride-to-be has always wanted to try her hand at a spot of pole dancing, which is apparently very good for one's core, not to mention likely to be hilarious when performed amid a gaggle of her best friends. If pole dancing doesn't appeal (or isn't enough!), you could also try belly dancing, cheerleading and burlesque. Or for the daring bride-to-be, perhaps a lesson in something like fire dancing is called for. Check what's available in the area.

HEN HACK

If you're renting a house on the outskirts of a city, why not see if you can afford to get one with a pool? You'll save money in the long run when you host your own **pool party**, with music and cocktails, a beach-themed barbecue, giant inflatables and games such as volleyball and limbo. If you can't find a house with a pool, you might find one with a hot tub, for all the hens to relax in after a hard night's partying.

EVENING ACTIVITIES

Cabaret – Head out to a steamy cabaret or raunchy burlesque show and enjoy some food and drink with entertainment on the side. Many hen party organisations offer packages in various locations, or you may be able to time your hen party to coincide with a burlesque show that's taking place in your area at a local theatre.

Shirtless butler – Now here's a hen party craze that has taken off in recent years: a young man, probably rather tanned, shiny and sporting a six-pack, will serve drinks to you and your friends wearing not very much at all. The company names in themselves are amusing and there are plenty to choose from: in the UK alone, you can find Butlers in the Buff, Hunks in Trunks, Butlers with Bums and Buff Naked Butlers, to name just a few.

Murder mystery – Seek out a nearby operator of murder mystery events for a weekend with a creepy edge. Many companies offer a personalised mystery, complete with in-jokes and other activities, all in a haunted house location.

Boat party – It goes without saying that you'll need a body of water nearby for this one, but it's a good shout if you have a bride-to-be who likes to party and you'd like to organise something a little bit different from her usual Saturday night out clubbing.

HEN HACK

If you're renting a house or cottage, bring the **karaoke** indoors. Ask one of the hens to bring karaoke equipment, such as SingStar. Whether staying in or warming up for a night out, you will save the cost of a private karaoke room and drinks out on the tiles. If you're feeling competitive, why not turn it into an X-Factor-style affair – appoint judges (those who can't/hate to sing and are happy to be on the other side of the table). Bring props – inflatable guitars, wigs, giant sunglasses, etc. You could even set up your own **photo booth**, using an iPad and remote, a curtain and a stool or two, in the corner of a room. Gather snaps of everyone with the props and print them out after the weekend as a memento for the bride-to-be.

ESSENTIAL KIT

★ Dancing shoes

★ Karaoke machine and props

★ Pool party accessories

★ iPad and remote for photo booth

FANCY DRESS IDEAS

★ Heroes and villains

★ Burlesque

★ Disney characters

★ 1980s/1990s

THEME: INTROVERT

'QUIET PEOPLE HAVE THE LOUDEST MINDS.'

★ *Stephen Hawking* ★

Perhaps the bride-to-be would prefer a day out rather than a weekend away. Maybe she'd rather sleep in her own bed and take part in some activities locally, or head to a quiet country cottage for a weekend of chilled-out fun. Is your bride-to-be creative? She might enjoy a pottery-painting, jewellery-designing or candle-making workshop. Or if she likes the outdoors, perhaps punting along a river or heading out on a nature walk could be the key to a successful weekend. Pre-wedding celebrations don't have to be all about downing shots surrounded by half-naked butlers; here are some suggestions for a more relaxed affair.

DAYTIME ACTIVITIES

Pottery painting – Many towns, cities and villages now have pottery-painting studios for parties for both children and adults. Not only do these provide an afternoon's entertainment, often in a private room, but each hen will get to take home her creation at the end of the day. Why not chip in for an extra item – perhaps a large plate or bowl – and take it in turns to sign it in different colours or write messages for the bride-to-be so she has a keepsake from the weekend.

Yoga retreat – If your bride-to-be is a yoga fan, she might be delighted with a surprise weekend to a yoga retreat. Budget permitting, you could even take her abroad to a beautiful and peaceful location where you can all practise mindful, gentle exercise in pleasant surroundings. Consider staying on an extra day to let your hair down once you've finished with the yoga. Alternatively, some companies offer laughter yoga workshops, which can be an amusing take on the practice for a yoga-mad hen and is guaranteed to lift everyone's spirits.

Vintage afternoon tea – If you don't feel like spending hours slaving over a hot oven, there are plenty of companies that will bring the vintage tea party to you, complete with vintage crockery, waitresses, cream teas, glasses of bubbly and special gifts for the hens. There's also the option to add vintage make-up or hair styling packages, with many styles to choose from. If your budget won't stretch or your bride-to-be prefers to take her afternoon tea in the present day, seek out a quaint local tearoom and book a table for the hens to spend the afternoon together.

Spa day – For the ultimate relaxing day out or weekend away, organise a spa retreat for your bride-to-be. This doesn't have to break the bank either, with spa day offers readily available via daily deal and dedicated websites. Do some research and you're sure to come up with a good deal.

HEN HACK

Save cash by doing something creative for free. Buy some **crafting kits** and create either badges, brooches, earrings or necklaces, fascinators or hair accessories for the big day, and enjoy an afternoon of crafting at a fraction of the price of an organised event. If you have an avid crafter in your circle of friends, even better, ask her to lead a session and offer some guidance.

EVENING ACTIVITIES

Pyjama party – For the ultimate in comfort, organise a pyjama party with drinks, snacks and games. Perhaps the bride-to-be would like nothing more than to watch her favourite films, while eating takeaway pizza and popcorn. Make it special by giving her a sash, or veil or customised T-shirt to wear while the party unfolds (she might hate the idea of this generally, but we're all friends here and no one is being paraded down an unfamiliar high street). Alternatively, throw a onesie party and offer a prize for the most ridiculous/best onesie.

Cupcake decorating – Does your bride-to-be religiously follow *The Great British Bake Off*? Perhaps a round of cupcake decorating could be in order to kick-start the weekend. Many companies offer organised cupcake-decorating classes for groups of hens. And the best thing about this activity is all the cakes you get to gorge on afterwards.

Movies and cocktails – For the movie buff bride-to-be, why not arrange a special film screening; you could even theme this so it fits in with her favourite genre. For example, if she loves chick flicks and rom-coms, serve bubbly and cocktails; if she loves horror films, serve Bloody Marys or Zombie cocktails and turn all the lights off; for action films, perhaps some chilli-infused mojitos and spicy snacks. You could even encourage the hens to dress up as characters from the film you're going to watch. Budget permitting, you could hire a screening room in which to watch the film, or choose the hen's house with the biggest TV or hire a projector. There are also companies that organise 'chick flicks and cocktails' evenings should you want someone else to sort it all out.

Dinner at the bride-to-be's favourite restaurant
– Perhaps you've opted for a day of activities locally and the bride-to-be will be laying down her head in her own bed this evening. Why not take her to her favourite restaurant or somewhere she's wanted to go to for ages and surprise her with the best table in the house? A nice touch would be the hens all chipping in to pay for her meal.

HEN HACK

To keep the costs down, instead of forking out for a cupcake-decorating class, you could do this yourself. Arrange for one (or several) of the hens to make a few batches of plain cupcakes – you could all chip in for the ingredients – and then buy some cheap piping bags (you can even use large zip-lock bags with a corner snipped off), cake sprinkles and edible glitter, etc. And there you have it – a DIY cupcake party.

ESSENTIAL KIT

★ Pyjamas/loungewear/yoga pants

★ Cake decorations

FANCY DRESS IDEAS

★ Colours

★ Gingham

★ Movie-inspired costumes

★ Or ditch this idea and let everyone be themselves!

THEME: QUIRKY

'BE YOURSELF.
EVERYONE ELSE
IS ALREADY TAKEN.'

★ *Oscar Wilde* ★

DAYTIME ACTIVITIES

Go to a music festival – The peak wedding season usually coincides with several major music festivals, so why not take the hen party to Glastonbury (or something a little easier to get hold of tickets for and perhaps more local to you)? There are festivals of all shapes and sizes, to fit every budget and music taste. You don't have to restrict yourself to local music festivals – you could also include this as part of a trip abroad if your budget will stretch.

Beer spa – For the beer-drinking bride-to-be who enjoys the odd spa day, what better than the Chodovar beer spa in the Czech Republic (www.chodovar.cz)? Not only will hens have the opportunity to taste the Chodovar Brewery's various offerings, but the highlight of the day will be relaxing in the hot beer bath, where each hen will have a glass that they can fill from the (cold) beer tap, and various treatments such as massages and hot grain packs are on offer, too.

'Thriller' dance class – For every bride-to-be who's watched the 'Thriller' video 400 times and always wished she could recreate it, this offers her a chance to do just that. Some companies offer a 'Thriller' dance class, but this would be just as easy to organise yourself. Learn the routine, perform it as one and why not dress up in zombie gear, complete with fake blood and fake scars just to make the experience more authentic.

Zombie experience/werewolf hunting – If your bride-to-be has a particular penchant for zombie films, you could arrange a terrifying day away for a zombie experience. Settings range from general darkness to shopping mall, asylum and urban battlefield, which all sound equally terrifying. Alternatively, you could take on the role of a werewolf hunter and prowl creepy surroundings, on the lookout for the canine howlers.

HEN HACK

Is the bride-to-be a music buff, but the party budget won't stretch to a **music festival**-fuelled weekend? Then why not create your own? Do any of the hens have friends in bands? If they're up for it, get them to play. Or just don your wellies and listen to music while playing games in a field, and create a music-festival vibe by camping out and spending an evening around the fire.

EVENING ACTIVITIES

Rubik's Cube party – Ask the hens to wear items of clothing in solid colours – white, red, blue, orange, yellow and green. They should wear a variety of items of clothing – stretchy/baggy stuff will work best so it'll fit everyone – gloves, legwarmers, coats, hats and scarves are all encouraged, too. Each person should wear at least one item of clothing in the above colours and the aim of the game is to spend the evening swapping clothes until you are dressed entirely in one colour.

Anything but clothes party – This party theme requires all guests to arrive wearing something other than clothes. This could entail creating an outfit from bin bags, cardboard boxes, tinsel and foliage, lampshade and curtains, or anything, in fact, that they can lay their hands on. Just as long as it wouldn't normally be classified as clothing, it's fair game.

Crystal Maze party – If your budget won't stretch to a fully organised day or evening of *Crystal Maze*-style activities, complete with a trip to the Crystal Dome, why not create your own? If you're staying in a cottage or rented house for the weekend, transform the rooms into the different zones (Aztec, Futuristic, Industrial and Medieval – it's amazing what you can do with tissue paper and streamers of varying colours) and organise games and puzzles in each accordingly. You could even get one of the hens to bring a desk fan and turn the bathroom into the Crystal Dome. Pick up some crystal paperweights in junk and charity shops to make the whole thing extra authentic.

ESSENTIAL KIT

★ Zombie make-up and fake blood
★ Household items and junk for fancy dress
★ Wellies
★ Dancing shoes

FANCY DRESS IDEAS

★ Tube stations
★ Band names
★ Lesser-known super-heroines (make up your own)
★ Serial killers/horror film characters
★ Tim Burton characters

LOCATIONS

UK

'WE DON'T TAKE OURSELVES AS SERIOUSLY AS SOME OTHER COUNTRIES DO.'

★ *Joan Collins* ★

TOP HEN PARTY DESTINATIONS IN THE UK

★ Aberdeen

★ Bath

★ Belfast

★ Birmingham

★ Brighton

★ Bristol

★ Blackpool

★ Cambridge

★ Cardiff

★ Chelsea

★ Chester

★ Edinburgh

★ Essex

★ Glasgow

★ London

★ Manchester

★ Newcastle

★ Newquay

★ Oxford

★ York

WHERE TO GO?

Take a look at the most popular destinations on the previous page and peruse the pages relating to the suggested themes. Marry the two together and you should be closer to finding a good fit. Whether the bride-to-be would prefer a city break, all-night clubbing, culture, nature and tranquillity, or a relaxing spa weekend are all things to consider. Ask the hens for some inspiration if you're feeling stumped and see where the suggestions lead you.

KEEP IT LOCAL

There are plenty of pros to keeping the activities local: depending on how local and if the budget is tight, people may be able to sleep in their own beds; those with children or other commitments may be able to dip in and out rather than missing out on the weekend altogether; those on a tight budget are more likely to be able to make it.

WHERE TO STAY?

Once you've decided on a location, think about the accommodation that would best suit your party. In a city centre you might want to rent a house and in the countryside you may prefer a cottage. Alternatively, you might want to stay in a hotel or B & B, or perhaps you'd rather stay at a campsite or in a forest – maybe a spot of glamping is up your street – or, if you're on a budget, there are youth hostels. Maybe you'd all rather take to the water and stay on a boat. Whatever you decide, there are plenty of websites out there that will make your job of finding the perfect place that much easier. Check the Resources section at the back of the book for more information.

HEN HACK

If you've rented a house or cottage for the weekend, on arrival, pop a box or two of fresh raspberries in the freezer and leave for a couple of hours. When all the guests have arrived and the first cork is popped, drop a frozen raspberry into the bottom of each glass, pour over the bubbly and serve. Blueberries, blackberries and grapes also work well.

WHEN TO GO?

Make sure the chosen location and the activities fit the weather. If your bride-to-be wants to go camping in Scotland, for example, a December hen party is out of the question. If you're planning a winter hen party, make sure people will still be able to get there whatever the weather – even if it snows.

ORGANISING THE HENS

★ Ensure all hens are aware of any extra items/props they need to bring or purchase themselves.

★ Work out how much everything is going to cost and let the hens know in advance how much money they will need to bring.

★ Make sure everyone is aware of any themes/fancy dress ideas.

★ Are you going anywhere that requires a dress code? Make sure all hens are aware of this.

★ Send out detailed instructions on how to get to the venue.

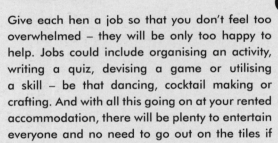

HEN HACK

Give each hen a job so that you don't feel too overwhelmed – they will be only too happy to help. Jobs could include organising an activity, writing a quiz, devising a game or utilising a skill – be that dancing, cocktail making or crafting. And with all this going on at your rented accommodation, there will be plenty to entertain everyone and no need to go out on the tiles if people don't want to!

ABROAD

**'I HAVEN'T BEEN
EVERYWHERE BUT
IT'S ON MY LIST.'**

★ *Susan Sontag* ★

TOP HEN PARTY DESTINATIONS OVERSEAS

★ Algarve

★ Amsterdam

★ Barcelona

★ Benidorm

★ Berlin

★ Dublin

★ Ibiza

★ Las Vegas

★ Madrid

★ Magaluf

★ Marbella

★ Milan

★ Prague

★ Valencia

WHERE TO GO?

Take a look at the most popular hen party destinations abroad (see left) for some inspiration and peruse the pages relating to the suggested themes. Marry the two together and you should be closer to finding a good fit. Does the bride-to-be want guaranteed sunshine? Does she want culture or the beach? Nightclubs and foam parties or natural beauty and tranquillity? Ask the other hens for some inspiration if you get stuck and together you'll come to the right decision.

TRAVEL ADVICE

For peace of mind, take a look at the FCO's Travel Advice page before you book any flights and make sure the location you've selected is a safe one (www.gov.uk/foreign-travel-advice).

WHERE TO STAY?

There are plenty of online resources to help you with this one, whether you opt for a villa, hotel or an apartment. Look at some of the many hotel deals websites for help and advice on all your accommodation needs.

WHEN TO GO?

When organising a hen party abroad, it's important to remember to keep costs down. As the plan starts to take shape, you don't want guests to start dropping out because the financial impact is spiralling out of control. For this reason it makes sense to avoid school holidays (and bank holidays, where possible), book flights and accommodation as far in advance as possible (and look out for discount codes and cashback offers – savings you can pass on to the hens) and, if possible, arrange to pay for the accommodation later to spread the cost over a few months.

THINGS TO CONSIDER

★ Are you travelling via a budget airline? If hold luggage costs extra, make sure each hen has told you whether they want to bring anything other than cabin baggage. Warn everyone that if they don't opt in now and then turn up with a big suitcase on the day, they will have to pay for it.

★ Remind all the hens to check their passport is in date – it's recommended that travellers have at least six months left on their passport before going abroad.

★ Make sure all the hens are aware of any props, items or outfits they need to bring with them and make sure everyone has room in their luggage.

★ Before you all head out, it's a sensible idea to organise a meeting place in case people get lost, or at least make sure everyone has the phone numbers of whoever are the key-holders of the accommodation.

★ Remind people to be sensible when it comes to their personal belongings – tourists are often targeted by pickpockets so everyone should carry around a photocopy of their passport (leaving the real thing back at the accommodation, unless you need it for ID and nothing else will do), make sure their bag doesn't gape open and generally have their wits about them.

★ Have a discussion about drink spiking and remind the hens not to leave their drinks unattended. Stick together!

★ Plan ahead and book restaurants, clubs and bars. Do some research and make sure there are plenty of places that accept large groups.

WHAT TO DO IF YOU LOSE YOUR PASSPORT

★ Before leaving the country, email a photo/scan of your passport to yourself. Take a photo of it with your phone so it's on there too.

★ Carry a printout of your travel itinerary, along with a passport photo and driver's licence – in case you need to acquire an emergency replacement passport.

★ Make sure you have the telephone number of your home country's embassy – in the event that you lose your passport, they will be able to help you.

★ If you believe you have lost your passport, don't panic. Check absolutely everywhere before raising the alarm. Go to the police if you believe your passport has been stolen.

THINGS TO MAKE AND DO

GAMES

'ALWAYS DO SOBER
WHAT YOU SAID YOU'D
DO DRUNK. THAT WILL
TEACH YOU TO KEEP
YOUR MOUTH SHUT.'

★ *Ernest Hemingway* ★

THINGS TO TAKE INTO CONSIDERATION

★ How well do the guests know each other? Will anyone mind sharing sensitive information with people they've just met?

★ Are there any family members present? Would the bride-to-be prefer things were kept 'clean'?

★ Are there many non-drinkers? If so, don't gear all the games around alcohol.

★ Make sure games are appropriate for the hens' ages and personality types. Don't, for example, make an introvert play strip poker and then drink a shot from a semi-naked butler's navel.

★ Is the venue suitable for the games in question?

★ How long will the games take and will they work with other activities planned?

DRINKING GAMES

Most likely – Guests sit in a circle and take it in turns to ask questions about who present would be most likely to do something. For example, 'Who would be most likely to get married in Las Vegas?', or 'Who would be most likely to try it on with a famous person in a bar?', or 'Who would be most likely to flake out and go to bed first?'. On the count of three, everyone should point at who they think would be most likely to do that. The person with the most fingers pointing at them has to take a drink or do a shot.

Banned words – Choose a word or phrase that is off limits for the night or the entire weekend, whatever you think will work best. This could be anything from 'bathroom' or 'kitchen' to the bride-to-be's partner's name or the word 'wedding'. Players will need to come up with alternative words for whatever has been banned and whoever drops the banned word over the course of the game needs to then take a drink or do a shot.

I have never... – In this game players sit in a circle and take it in turns to admit to something they have never done. This can be hugely embarrassing or just something like 'I have never been to China' or 'I have never been on a motorbike', and whoever has done that thing must take a drink or do a shot. In games like this where a lot of drinking is likely to be involved, you're better off setting the drink people need to take as either a sip or two fingers.

Name that drink – Here's one to get the bride-to-be's tastebuds working hard. Organise for each hen to bring an alcoholic drink that the bride-to-be might associate with that guest, be it her regular tipple or perhaps a drink that is attached to a memory or an entertaining story. Blindfold the bride-to-be and make her try each of the drinks and guess who has provided what. (She doesn't have to drink the whole drink – that might get a bit messy!).

Where's the water? – Take ten identical shot glasses and fill half of them with water and half with vodka. The hens must take it in turns to choose a glass and drink the contents. Someone needs to be in charge for this one and to avoid the hens seeing you pour out the drinks, perhaps you could get them to all face the other way or, even better, to play the game blindfolded and choose the glasses by number.

Roxanne – One of the best drinking games ever concocted. For this one all you'll need is a full glass, a chair/sitting place each and 'Roxanne' by The Police at the ready, either via a stereo or, if desperate, via your mobile phone. Split the players into two teams – one team is assigned the lyric 'Roxanne' and the other team takes 'red light'. Whenever Sting sings 'Roxanne', the team of the same name must stand up and take a drink and whenever he sings 'red light' the other team must get up from their seat and take a swig. Best played only once of an evening.

Keep a straight face – Hand out some scraps of paper and pens and get all players to write down something beginning with 'I have…' or 'I am…' or 'I will…', etc. The aim of the game is to make these as ridiculous as possible. Fold up all bits of paper and place in a bowl. The players should then take it in turns to take from the bowl and read out whatever is written on the piece of paper, all the while keeping a straight face. Whoever smiles or giggles while reading from their piece of paper must take a drink or do a shot.

MORE DRINKING GAMES

★ Beer pong (see page 37)

★ Pass the parcel (with a twist)

★ Spin the bottle

★ Shot roulette

★ Call my bluff

★ Card games

NON-DRINKING GAMES

Name in a hat – Split the party into two teams and hand each player three scraps of paper and a pen. Ask each hen to write down the name of a person – real or fictional, alive or dead – fold it up and put it in a large bowl. No one must reveal their name to anyone else. This game consists of three rounds, in which players from each team take it in turns to take names from the hat, offer clues to their teammates and allow them to guess the name in question. Each player has a 30-second slot and teams should alternate as it is important that everyone is listening the whole time. Here's the twist. The round is over when all names have been removed from the hat – then they must be refolded and placed back in the bowl. In round one you can use as many words as you like to describe the person as long as you do not actually say their name; in round two you may use only three words to describe the person; and in round three you may only describe that person using noises or gestures. Players are allowed to pass, but each correct guess equals a point, which will be added up at the end to determine who has won.

Sticky-note game – Write the name of a famous person – real or fictional, alive or dead – on a Sticky note and stick to the forehead of the person opposite you. Once everyone has a name stuck to their forehead the game can begin. Players take it in turns to ask questions about the person whose name is attached to their forehead. They can ask as many questions as they like until they get a 'no' answer and then the questioning moves round to the next player. The last person to guess correctly loses the game.

Toilet paper couture – Split the hens into teams and supply them each with a couple of rolls of toilet paper. The teams should each choose a 'model' and they then have five minutes to create a wedding dress entirely out of toilet paper. Choose someone to judge who has created the most beautiful dress.

Name that food/drink – Place various foods and drinks in bowls and cups on a table. Someone will need to be in charge. Blindfold the players and get them to taste the various foodstuffs and beverages, guessing what they are. Whoever guesses the most correctly wins the game.

How many pegs...? – Sort of like human Buckaroo, see how many pegs you can attach to other hens without them realising. Whoever secures the most pegs wins the game. This is a good one to play alongside another game, so everyone is distracted and so hopefully not realising when they're being pegged! Buy pegs in a selection of sizes and assign a points system, so giant pegs score the highest and miniature pegs score less. Hand out the pegs and make sure everyone writes their initials on each peg in their collection so points can be tallied up at the end.

Name that baby – Ask each hen to bring a photo of themselves as a baby or small child (ask a member of the bride-to-be's family to provide one of her). Number them all and ask the hens to write down which hen they think each childhood photo belongs to.

The handbag game – Ask each hen to place three items from their handbag into a larger bag. Hens should then take it in turns to draw out an item and guess who it belongs to. Points should be rewarded for correct answers and whoever has the most points at the end wins. Alternatively, you could ask each hen to place just one item into a bag and ask the bride-to-be to guess who owns what.

MORE NON-DRINKING GAMES

★ Pin the tie on the groom

★ Truth or dare

★ Scavenger/treasure hunt

★ Charades

★ Wedding Pictionary

OUT AND ABOUT?

Why not present the bride-to-be with a dozen roses and dare her to hand them out over the course of the evening to various people, in exchange for a kiss. This is probably not one for shrinking violets.

GAMES ALL ABOUT THE BRIDE-TO-BE

Mr & Mrs – This one takes a bit of organisation but is well worth it. Come up with a list of questions about the bride-to-be's partner and ask them to provide the answers. Even better – film it on your phone (or ask the partner to) and get someone to bring a laptop/tablet or pipe it into the TV, so you can play their responses to her at the hen party. Ask the bride-to-be each question, wait for her response and then play her partner's response. If she answers incorrectly she should take a drink or do a shot. If she's getting loads of them wrong, be kind and let her nominate another hen to do a shot for her!

Memory bag – Ask each hen to bring an item or prop that is likely to evoke a memory relating to their friendship with the bride-to-be. All items should be placed in a bag and then removed one at a time by the bride-to-be while she guesses who placed it there and tells the story of the memory.

How well do you know the bride-to-be? – Turning the previous game around, you could organise for the bride-to-be to answer a list of questions about herself (and film her answering them) and then ask the hens to take it in turns answering the questions. Whoever answers incorrectly must have a drink or do a shot.

KEEPSAKE FOR THE BRIDE-TO-BE

'SOME PEOPLE GO TO PRIESTS; OTHERS TO POETRY; I TO MY FRIENDS.'

★ *Virginia Woolf* ★

Scrapbook – An oldie but a goodie: ask hens to bring photos of themselves with the bride-to-be and invite them to slope off to a quiet spot at some point over the weekend to help build the scrapbook. This can include photos, messages, stickers and whatever else you like to make the pages colourful.

Lipstick canvas – Buy a blank canvas and ask all the hens to pucker up and plant a lipstick kiss on to it, signing their name next to it and writing a personal message. In case there are no lipstick wearers among the hens, buy a few cheap ones in different shades to create a colourful collage of kisses for your bride-to-be.

Hen party guestbook – Buy a blank guestbook and ask hens to sign it over the course of the weekend, writing messages about the bride-to-be and the fun they've had at her hen party. There will no doubt be a few pages left at the end – ask the bride-to-be if you can borrow the book after the hen party and fill these empty pages with pictures of the weekend.

Knitted blanket – Hopefully some of your hens are able to knit and if they can't the ones who can will be able to teach them. This can either be incorporated into the day as an activity or can be done prior to the hen party. Ask all hens (and any other family members who want to join in) to knit a square to a certain size, in whatever colour they choose and ask the most creative of your group to stitch them all together into a wedding blanket.

Wedding kit – Create a box of surprises for your bride-to-be to open on her wedding night. This could include luxury bath items, champagne, chocolates, massage oils and, depending on your budget, maybe even silk dressing gowns embroidered with the bride and groom's initials or names. Include notes from the hens or all sign a big card with messages referring to how she might be feeling on her wedding night.

SOME MORE IDEAS

★ Ask each hen to write a 'recipe for a great marriage' on a wooden spoon and sign it.

★ Design a T-shirt for the bride-to-be (or in fact everyone there that weekend).

★ Design a sash for the bride-to-be to wear that weekend and keep afterwards.

★ Create a mixtape/CD/MP3 playlist of songs that are meaningful to the bride-to-be or her relationship with her partner.

★ Create a timeline or scrapbook of the bride-to-be's relationship with her partner.

★ Create or buy a lucky charm that she can carry with her or wear on her wedding day.

★ Buy or create a hen party mascot that the bride-to-be must carry around with her all weekend and keep once the party is over.

COCKTAIL RECIPES

'I LIKE TO HAVE A MARTINI,
TWO AT THE VERY MOST.
AFTER THREE I'M UNDER THE
TABLE, AFTER FOUR
I'M UNDER MY HOST.'

★ *Dorothy Parker* ★

It wouldn't be a hen party without a glass or two of something brightly coloured garnished with an umbrella or half a mint plant/far too much fruit. Whether you're after booze-filled creations or something lighter, cleaner and non-alcoholic, read on for all your hen weekend imbibing needs. All recipes are for one serving unless otherwise indicated, so feel free to multiply the quantities in order to create pitchers full of cocktail fun for your group of hens!

FROZEN MARGARITA

INGREDIENTS

50 ml tequila
25 ml lime juice
12.5 ml triple sec
Ice
Slice of lime

METHOD

Mix all ingredients in a blender with half a cup of ice. Blend at low speed until slushy and then serve with a slice of lime.

STRAWBERRY DAIQUIRI JELLY SHOTS

INGREDIENTS
(makes 10 large or 20 small shots)

1 packet of strawberry jelly
250 ml Malibu or other coconut rum
250 ml water
10–20 plastic shot glasses
Squirty cream

METHOD

Boil the water, stir in the jelly cubes until dissolved and leave to cool to room temperature. This is very important – if you add the Malibu to hot water or cook it, your shots will lose alcohol content. Once the jelly and water mixture has cooled, add the Malibu and stir. Pour the mixture into the shot glasses set on a tray and place in the fridge for a few hours. Allow an hour or so longer than the instructions given on the jelly packet, as the added alcohol will slow down the setting process. Serve with a dollop of squirty cream on top of each shot.

MIXED BERRY MOJITO

INGREDIENTS

1 tbsp fresh blackberries
1 tbsp fresh raspberries
3 mint leaves
1 tbsp sugar
1 large lime wedge
50 ml white rum
Ice
Soda water

METHOD

Place the blackberries, raspberries, mint leaves and sugar into a tall glass, squeeze the lime wedge over the top and pour in the rum. Muddle the mixture together until the fruit is broken up and the mint bruised. Use the back of a spoon if you don't have the appropriate mixologist's tool. Add ice and fill the remainder of the glass with soda water. Stir gently to combine and garnish with more mint leaves and a slice of lime if desired.

CHERRY WHISKEY SMASH

INGREDIENTS

2 fresh cherries
20 ml fresh lemon juice
6 fresh mint leaves
1 wedge orange
1 tsp sugar syrup
50 ml cherry bourbon whiskey
Ice

METHOD

Place the cherries, lemon juice and mint leaves into a cocktail shaker, squeeze over the juice from the orange wedge and muddle. You can use the back of a spoon to do this. Add the sugar syrup, cherry bourbon and a handful of ice and shake hard. Strain the cocktail into a tumbler filled with crushed ice and garnish with a mint sprig and a fresh cherry.

APPLETINI

INGREDIENTS

25 ml vodka
25 ml apple schnapps
Splash of dry vermouth
Ice
Slice of apple

METHOD

Place the vodka, apple schnapps and vermouth into a cocktail shaker with a handful of ice and give it a good shake. Then strain into a chilled Martini glass and garnish with a slice of apple.

SANGRIA

INGREDIENTS
(serves 5–6)

750 ml Spanish red wine – go for Grenache, Tempranillo
or Rioja (and don't spend too much on it, you're about
to water it down!)

250 ml orange juice

500 ml lemonade

250 ml brandy, optional

Lots of sliced citrus fruit – oranges,
lemons and limes

Ice

METHOD

Place a couple of handfuls of ice into a large jug and
add the fruit slices. Then pour over the red wine, orange
juice, lemonade and brandy (if desired). Taste, and add
more wine, juice or lemonade if desired or you feel
it needs it. Stir well and pour into individual glasses
(large wine glasses work well). Make sure each serving
includes plenty of sliced fruit.

PINK GIN FIZZ

INGREDIENTS

25 ml gin (or twice this, depending on your preference for strength of drink!)
100 ml pink grapefruit juice
Squeeze of lime
150 ml tonic water
Ice
Slice of pink grapefruit

METHOD

Add the gin, pink grapefruit juice and squeeze of lime juice to a cocktail shaker and mix well. Pour into a tall glass over ice and top with tonic water. Garnish with a slice of pink grapefruit if desired.

STRAWBERRY MIMOSA

INGREDIENTS

50 ml strawberry puree
100 ml champagne, Prosecco, cava or
other sparkling white wine
1 fresh strawberry

METHOD

Pour the strawberry puree into a champagne flute and top with your white sparkling wine of choice. Garnish with a strawberry.

NON-ALCOHOLIC COCKTAILS

Who says the drinkers get all the nice cocktails? Push the boat out and make a bit of an effort for the non-drinkers in the house. It's likely there will be a few – be they pregnant or only visiting for the day and needing to drive home, or simply not bothered about the booze. No one wants to be the odd one out so make sure everyone has a glass of something special in their hand.

MANGO FIZZ

INGREDIENTS

125 ml ginger ale
5 mint leaves
25 ml mango puree
25 ml lime juice
25 ml sugar syrup
Crushed ice
Sprig of mint

METHOD

Place the mint, sugar syrup, lime and mango puree in a tall glass and muddle gently. Add a handful or two of crushed ice, until the glass is two-thirds full, and top up with ginger ale. Give the whole thing a good stir, add more crushed ice if needed and garnish with a sprig of mint.

VIRGIN MOJITO

INGREDIENTS

5 mint leaves
1 tbsp fresh lime juice
1 tsp sugar
Crushed ice
250 ml ginger ale, soda water or lemonade
Sprig of mint

METHOD

Place the mint leaves, lime juice and sugar in a tall glass and muddle well. Add a handful or two of crushed ice and top with ginger ale, soda water or lemonade, depending on how sweet you want the end result to be. Give the whole lot a good stir and then top with more crushed ice if needed and a sprig of mint to garnish.

PARTY SNACKS AND HANGOVER CURES

'GREASE IS THE ONLY CURE FOR A HANGOVER.'

★ *Cameron Diaz* ★

BREAKFAST BURRITOS

INGREDIENTS (makes 4)

4 flour or corn tortillas
6 eggs
100 g cheddar
6 tbsp milk
1 tbsp butter
3 red peppers, roasted, skinned and chopped (from a jar)
6 piquanté peppers
Handful of baby spinach leaves
Salt and pepper
Hot pepper sauce

METHOD

Beat the eggs in a bowl and add the milk. Season with salt and pepper and whisk. Melt the butter in a frying pan, until it starts to foam, then add the egg mixture. Cook the eggs to your liking and remove from the heat. Put the roasted red peppers, chopped piquanté peppers and spinach into a bowl and mix well. Warm the tortillas and place one on each plate. Spread a quarter of the grated cheese over the tortilla, top with a spoonful of the pepper and spinach mixture and add a quarter of the egg, before adding a dash of hot pepper sauce and rolling up the tortilla into a tube. Now eat and banish that hangover!

EASY FRENCH TOAST

INGREDIENTS (serves 12)

12 slices thick white bread
4 eggs
175 ml milk
3 tbsp soft light brown sugar
1 tsp ground nutmeg
1 tbsp ground cinnamon
Icing sugar to serve
Crispy bacon, blueberries and maple syrup, optional

METHOD

Beat the eggs in a bowl, then add the milk, brown sugar and nutmeg and stir well. Soak each slice of bread in the mixture until saturated. Lightly oil a large frying pan and brown the slices on each side. Serve hot, dusted with icing sugar and cinnamon, with crispy bacon or blueberries and maple syrup if desired.

PIZZA PINWHEELS

INGREDIENTS (serves 8–10)

FOR THE PASTRY (you can buy ready-made pastry if pushed for time):

250 g self-raising flour
50 g margarine
150 g milk

FOR THE TOPPINGS:

100 g grated mozzarella
50 g grated cheddar
200 g tomato puree
1 tsp dried oregano
1 tsp dried basil
Other toppings of your choice: pepperoni slices,
    peppers, onions, sweetcorn, etc.
Cooking oil

METHOD

Preheat oven to 220°C (200°C fan oven). Sieve the flour into a mixing bowl and rub in the margarine until the mixture looks like breadcrumbs. Add the milk and combine to a soft dough. Dust a surface with flour, transfer the dough and knead gently. Using a rolling pin, roll the dough out to roughly the size of an A4 piece of paper. Spread tomato puree over the pastry, sprinkle on cheese, herbs and any other toppings and carefully roll up the dough into a long tube. Slice into 8–10 pieces and place on a baking tray. Dab the pinwheels with a little oil (if you have a spray can of oil, even better) and bake for 10–15 minutes until golden.

CHEESY SHARING LOAF

INGREDIENTS

1 large crusty white loaf of bread (tiger bread is best)
115 g butter, melted
115 g pesto or pureed garlic
150 g cheddar, grated
150 g mozzarella, grated
50 g parmesan, grated

METHOD

Preheat the oven to 190°C (170°C fan oven) . Using a serrated knife, make one-inch diagonal cuts into the loaf, leaving the bottom intact, then repeat this action in the opposite direction. Melt the butter in a saucepan and pour into the gaps in the bread, distributing evenly. Now spread the pesto or garlic evenly along the gaps in the bread. Next, mix all the grated cheese together in a bowl. Place the loaf on to a large piece of foil and stuff the cheese into the gaps in the bread. Wrap the load in the foil and bake for 15 minutes. Open the foil and bake for a further 10 minutes. Allow the loaf to sit for 10 minutes before serving. This is the perfect finger food, so let guests serve themselves, although you may want to keep a stack of paper napkins handy as it can get a bit messy!

STUFFED SWEET POTATO SKINS

INGREDIENTS (makes 8)

4 sweet potatoes
4 strips streaky bacon
100 g mozzarella, grated
100 g cheddar, grated
60 ml milk

1 tbsp olive oil
Sour cream
Chives
Salt and pepper

METHOD

Preheat the oven to 200°C (180°C fan oven). Pierce the sweet potatoes a few times with a fork and place on a baking tray. Cook for 50 minutes and leave to cool. Once cooled, cut potatoes in half lengthways and scoop out the flesh, leaving only a thin layer of potato inside, and place flesh in a bowl. Return potato skins to baking tray, drizzle with olive oil and bake for 10 minutes. Add the milk, salt and pepper to the potato flesh and mix well. Fill the potato skins with the mixture and top with a generous amount of cheese. Bake these at 200°C (180°C fan oven) for 15 minutes. While these are cooking, grill the bacon until crispy and crumble into a bowl. Once the cheese has melted on the potato skins, remove from oven and top with bacon bits. Serve with sour cream topped with chopped chives.

RESOURCES

'BEFORE ANYTHING ELSE,
PREPARATION IS KEY
TO SUCCESS.'

★ *Alexander Graham Bell* ★

ACTIVITIES/ ENTERTAINMENT A–Z

Aerial acrobatics: www.flyingfantastic.co.uk

Boat party: www.chillisauce.co.uk

Cabaret/burlesque: www.adoniscabaret.co.uk, www.houseofburlesque.co.uk, www.ticketmaster.co.uk

Cocktail making: www.revolution-bars.co.uk/ hen-party, www.jaminns.co.uk

Dance classes: www.bijouxhenparties.co.uk

Fascinator making: www.craftsandgiggles.com/ fascinator-making, www.glamhatters.com

Food festivals: www.thefestivalcalendar.co.uk/ food-festivals-calendar.php

Jewellery making: www.handmadehen.co.uk

Karaoke: www.luckyvoice.com

Kimono party: www.takayo.co.uk

Life drawing: www.henswithpens.com

Makeover party: www.lipstickandgunpowder.com

RESOURCES

Murder mystery: www.murdermysteryevents.com,
www.clearcutweekends.co.uk,
www.hauntedmysteryweekend.co.uk

Music festivals: www.thefestivalcalendar.co.uk,
www.festicket.com/festivals

Paintballing: www.ukpaintball.co.uk.

Perfume making: www.theperfumestudio.com

Recording studio experience: www.studiostars.co.uk,
www.gohen.com/activities/recording.asp

Scavenger hunt: www.xmarksthespot.co.uk

Shirtless butler: www.butlersinthebuff.co.uk,
www.hunksintrunks.co.uk, www.butlerswithbums.com,
www.buffnakedbutlers.co.uk

Snow domes: www.skiclub.co.uk/skiclub/
infoandadvice/uksnowsports/ukslopesmap.aspx

Spas: www.groupon.co.uk, www.livingsocial.com,
www.spabreaks.com, www.spaseekers.com

Tank Driving: www.tankdriving.co.uk/experiences/
stag-and-hen-parties

Treasure hunt: www.adventureconnections.co.uk

Vintage knicker making: www.sewretro.co.uk/parties

Vintage-themed tea parties/makeovers:
www.hopeandgloriousvintage.co.uk,
www.teaandtrim.com

Walking/hiking: www.nationaltrail.co.uk, www.walkengland.org.uk

Werewolf hunting: www.gohen.com, www.chillisauce.co.uk

Wine/gin tasting: www.sugarandyeast.co.uk, www.darlinghens.co.uk, www.clearcutweekends.co.uk

Zombie experience: www.zombieexperiences.co.uk

ACCOMMODATION

Boats: www.waterwaysholidays.com, www.drifters.co.uk

Campsites: www.coolcamping.co.uk

Center Parcs: www.centerparcs.co.uk

Group accommodation: www.henheaven.co.uk, www.homeaway.co.uk, www.groupaccommodation.com, www.airbnb.com, www.bigholidayhouse.com and www.henpartyvenues.co.uk

Hotels/B & Bs: www.hotels.com, www.trivago.co.uk

Youth hostels: www.yha.org.uk

TRAVEL

Eurostar Snow Trains: www.eurostar.com/uk-en/
train/france/ski-train

If you're interested in finding out more about our books, find us on Facebook at **Summersdale Publishers** and follow us on Twitter at **@Summersdale**.

www.summersdale.com